SimplyHealthful

Cakes

THE SIMPLY HEALTHFUL SERIES

Simply Healthful Cakes by Donna Deane and Minnie Bernardino
Simply Healthful Fish by David Ricketts and Susan McQuillan
Simply Healthful Pasta Salads by Andrea Chesman

PHOTOGRAPHY CREDITS

Kirk McKoy: front cover, 27, 39, 40, 45, 52, 57, 65, 87, 92
Randy Leffingwell: 15, 16, 21, 23, 35, 61
Con Keyes: 28
Al Seib: 49
Jim Mendenhall: 73
Tony Barnard: 79
Robert Durell: 80

Tableware and accessories courtesy of
Judie and Alan Schoening of Schoening Enterprises
Franklin Pentecoste of Vest & Associates
Debra and Heino Egert of Rosenthal USA.

Cakes

Delicious New Low-Fat Recipes

By Donna Deane & Minnie Bernardino

CHAPTERS™

CHAPTERS PUBLISHING LTD., SHELBURNE, VERMONT 05482

Published by
Chapters Publishing Ltd.
2031 Shelburne Road
Shelburne, Vermont 05482

Library of Congress Cataloguing-in-Publication Data

Deane, Donna
Simply healthful cakes / by Donna Deane and Minnie Bernardino
p. cm. -- (Simply healthful)
Includes index.
ISBN 1-881527-07-7 : $9.95
1. Cake. 2. Cookery, (Fruit) I. Bernardino, Minnie
II. Title. III. Series: Simply healthful series.
TX771.D43 1993
641.8'653—dc20
92-40573
CIP

Trade distribution by
Firefly Books Ltd.
250 Sparks Avenue
Willowdale, Ontario
Canada M2H 2S4

Printed and bound in Canada by
Friesen Printers
Altona, Manitoba

Designed by Hans Teensma/Impress, Inc.

Contents

Introduction

"Avoid animal fats. Who needs them?"
—Marilyn Monroe

THIS BOOK BEGAN with a laugh. A year and a half ago, we came across a small article suggesting that it was possible to bake brownies without butter. An intriguing idea, but the author was suggesting that we simply use prunes instead. That seemed very funny. "Nonsense," we said to each other. And then we decided to try it. After all, what if it worked?

At the time, baking great cakes without fat seemed a bit like perpetual motion—appealing but impossible. While everybody loves cake, all the things that go into cakes are also the things you aren't supposed to eat. Even the people who don't mind the calories in cake are inevitably wary of the health implications of eating massive amounts of butter, eggs and cream. So we baked the brownies. We used our favorite recipe and simply replaced the fat with an equal amount of a puree made out of dried prunes. We expected to open the oven and find a desiccated mess. But instead we opened it and discovered . . . brownies.

They weren't the best brownies we'd ever eaten—they tasted a bit fruity—but they were good enough to fool most people into thinking they really were indulging in a guilty pleasure. And they were almost fat-free! We were shocked and pleased. "If that works," we said to each other, "maybe we could bake a white cake using dried apricots instead of prunes." We tried that and discovered that the resulting cake was a bit tough, but good enough to make us want to try again. And again. By the time we came up with an acceptable cake, we were getting a little tired of soaking dried fruit and pureeing it. We hit on the idea of using baby food purees. We weren't sure it would work, but it did. Was it, we wondered, possible to use fruits other than prunes and apricots? Since we had moved on to baby food, it was easy to experiment. We quickly found that we could substitute virtually any fruit puree for fat in a cake recipe.

This discovery led us to wonder why the fruit puree worked. A call to food-science writer Harold McGee yielded some answers. According to McGee, fruit purees function much like fat, tenderizing the dough by diluting the chewy structure of the gluten. Because of their viscosity and body, fruit purees can participate in the structure of the cake without strengthening the gluten.

Fortified with a bona fide scientific explanation of the principle, we went on baking. Within a month of taking the first batch of prune brownies out of the oven, we had baked almost 50 cakes, analyzing each one. Then we let them sit a day and tasted them again. After the initial euphoria of the discovery wore off, we had to admit that they were good—for low-fat cakes. But we didn't want "diet desserts," we wanted desserts that anybody could serve with pride. To get really good cakes, we realized, would require more than just replacing the fat with fruit purees. It would require a new baking formula.

Finally, we narrowed our selection to eight perfected cakes. From simple everyday cakes we moved on to more glamorous party cakes, cheesecakes and tortes—both traditional desserts and new ones. We discovered other ways to trade fat, using fat-free dairy and egg substitutes. Beaten egg whites replaced some or all of the egg yolks, creating fluffy texture.

When we published the recipes in our column in the *Los Angeles Times*, we found that our work had been worth it. Our readers were thrilled. "You've changed my life," wrote one; "I thought good desserts had gone out of my life forever." "Give us more!" wrote another. And so, for a year, we did just that. And the longer we worked on low-fat baking, the more demanding we became about the results. By the end of the year, we were baking cakes with just a gram or two of fat.

Because the chemistry of low-fat baking is very different from that of regular baking, we were never quite sure what would happen in the oven. And because we were using so many new ingredients, there were no set guidelines. We found that the order of the ingredients can be crucial. How the batter is mixed is equally important. A slight variation in oven temperature can mean the difference between a great cake and a mediocre one. A small change in pan size can also make an enormous difference. We were often forced to rework a recipe eight or ten times until we were satisfied with the result.

As time went on, our cakes got better and better. We knew we had really succeeded the day a photographer dropped into the kitchen and cut himself an enormous piece of a chocolate cake we were testing for a holiday story. It was anything but low-fat—loaded with butter, eggs and chocolate. He polished off the piece, put down his plate and said, "You guys have really got these low-fat recipes down! This is almost as good as that low-fat lemon cake you baked last week." When someone prefers a cake with 185 calories and 2 grams of fat per serving to one with 750 calories and 36 grams of fat, you know you're onto something.

As Marilyn Monroe would say, "Who needs animal fats?"

———————

The following guidelines were used in determining the nutritional analysis of each recipe:

◆ When a recipe offers a choice within the ingredient list, the first ingredient listed is the one represented in the nutritional analysis.

◆ When an ingredient is listed as "optional," it is not included in the analysis.

Glossary

Nonfat Egg Substitute (such as Fleischmann's Egg Beaters): A frozen liquid-egg product made of 99 percent egg whites, plus trace amounts of corn oil, emulsifiers and stabilizers, fortified with vitamins and minerals. Once defrosted, the product has the consistency and color of stirred eggs.

One-fourth cup replaces 1 whole egg in most recipes, and 1 egg yolk in recipes calling for up to 2 egg yolks. Compared to 1 egg, which contains 70 calories, 5 grams of fat and 240 milligrams of cholesterol, the substitute contains 25 calories, no fat and no cholesterol. The nonfat product will not whip or foam and therefore does not increase the volume of baked goods. (Another product, called Simply Eggs, made from whole eggs with reduced cholesterol and fat, has the whipping property of real eggs.) All of the recipes in this book can be made with regular eggs; follow the equivalents given.

Frozen egg substitute comes in 8-ounce cartons and is found in the freezer section of the supermarket.

Instant Nonfat Dry Milk (such as Carnation Instant Nonfat Dry Milk): Dried granules made from whole milk that have been processed to remove almost all water and butterfat; fortified with vitamins A and D. Compared to 1 cup of whole milk, which contains 159 calories, 8.5 grams of fat and 33 milligrams of cholesterol, 1 cup of reconstituted nonfat dry milk (5 tablespoons powdered milk per cup of water) contains 80 calories, 0.2 grams fat and 5 milligrams of cholesterol.

Added dry to cakes, instant nonfat dry milk enriches flavor and nutritive value. It comes in 9.6-ounce cartons and may be found on the dry-goods shelf of the supermarket by the coffee and canned milk.

Nonfat Milk: Pasteurized, homogenized and enriched with vitamins A and D, nonfat milk is made from whole milk with 98 to 99 percent of the butterfat removed. Compared to 1 cup of whole milk, which contains 159 calories, 8.5 grams of fat and 33 milligrams of cholesterol, nonfat milk contains 90 calories, less than 1 gram of fat and 5 milligrams of cholesterol.

Nonfat milk does not have the creaminess of whole milk but provides acceptable consistency and flavor in such low-fat preparations as cakes, custard sauces and flan. It is available in refrigerated dairy cases.

Low-Fat Whipped Topping (such as Cool Whip Lite Whipped Topping): Made to taste and look like sweetened whipped cream; made from skim milk, corn syrup, hydrogenated oils and emulsifiers, it contains one-third less fat than regular frozen whipped topping. Compared to 1 cup of heavy whipped cream, which contains 419 calories and 89.5 grams of fat, low-fat whipped topping contains 128 calories and about 16 grams of fat.

Once defrosted, the topping may be used like whipped cream in many dessert recipes. Available in 8- and 12-ounce cartons, it is found in the freezer case.

Low-Fat Butter Spread: Made partly with butter, and with liquid corn oil, partially hydrogenated corn oil and emulsifiers, it contains one-third to one-half less fat than butter, and 85 percent less cholesterol. Compared to 1 tablespoon butter, which contains 102 calories, 11.5 grams of fat and 31 milligrams of cholesterol, low-fat butter spread contains 60 calories, 6 grams of fat and 3.3 milligrams of cholesterol.

Canola oil-based margarine may be used instead, but the flavor will be inferior. Low-fat butter spread comes in 16-ounce carton tubs or stick form and is available in the dairy case of the supermarket.

Fat-Free Cottage Cheese (such as Knudson Free Nonfat Cottage Cheese): Dry-curd cottage cheese with a creamy consistency, made from cultured nonfat milk with modified food starch and cream flavor added. Compared to 1 cup large-curd creamed cottage cheese (4 percent fat), which contains 259 calories, 9.5 grams of fat and 34 milligrams of cholesterol, fat-free cottage cheese contains 140 calories, no fat and 5 milligrams of cholesterol.

Nonfat Sour Cream Substitute (such as Knudson Free Light Sour Cream Substitute): Thick and silky smooth like sour cream, this substitute is made of cultured pasteurized nonfat milk with modified food starch, stabilizers and vitamin A added. Compared to 1 tablespoon regular sour cream, which contains 30 calories, 3 grams of fat and 5 milligrams of cholesterol, nonfat sour cream substitute contains 9 calories, no fat and no cholesterol.

Nonfat sour cream substitute is available in 16-ounce tubs in the supermarket dairy case. Nonfat plain yogurt may be substituted.

Light Cream Cheese (available in store brand): Made of salted pasteurized cream with cheese cultures added. Compared to 1 ounce regular cream cheese, which contains 100 calories and 10 grams fat, light cream cheese contains 80 calories and 7 grams of fat. It is available in 8-ounce blocks in the supermarket dairy case.

Fat-Free Ice Cream: Nonfat frozen dessert made of skim milk, sweeteners, egg whites and stabilizers. Compared to 1 cup regular vanilla ice cream, which contains 175 calories, 12 grams of fat and 44 milligrams of cholesterol, fat-free ice cream contains 90 calories, less than 1 gram of fat and no cholesterol.

Fat-free ice cream is available in quart or half-gallon sizes in the supermarket freezer case. Frozen yogurt may be substituted.

Spring Cakes

Chocolate Cloud

CAKE

	Butter or nonstick cooking spray for preparing pans
2	cups all-purpose flour
2	cups sugar
1	cup unsweetened cocoa powder
2	teaspoons baking soda
1	teaspoon baking powder
¼	teaspoon salt
4	jars (2½ ounces each) baby food prune puree
1	cup nonfat milk
½	cup thawed frozen nonfat egg substitute (equivalent to 2 eggs)
2	teaspoons vanilla
2	tablespoons instant espresso coffee powder
1	cup boiling water

SEVEN-MINUTE FROSTING (OPTIONAL)

1	tablespoon instant espresso coffee powder
¼	cup hot water
3	egg whites, slightly below room temperature
1½	cups light brown sugar, packed
1	teaspoon cream of tartar
1	teaspoon vanilla

1. Prepare Cake: Preheat oven to 350 degrees F. Lightly butter bottom and sides of two 9-inch round layer cake pans or spray with nonstick cooking spray.

2. Sift together flour, sugar, cocoa powder, baking soda, baking powder and salt into large mixing bowl. Stir until blended. Add prune puree, nonfat milk, egg substitute and vanilla and stir just until blended.

3. Combine espresso powder and boiling water and stir until dissolved. Stir into batter until blended. Pour batter into prepared pans.

4. Bake for 30 to 35 minutes, or until wooden pick inserted in center comes out clean. Let cakes cool in pans 10 minutes. Invert onto wire rack to cool.

(continued on page 14)

This chocolate cake is made with pureed prunes, but prunes aren't what you taste. Although we aren't going to pretend this is the richest chocolate cake you can make, we've sampled enough low-fat chocolate cakes to know that it is straightforward and very satisfying.

5. Prepare Seven-Minute Frosting, if using: Dissolve espresso powder in hot water. Combine egg whites, brown sugar, coffee mixture and cream of tartar in top of double boiler placed over very gently simmering water. Beat with mixer until frosting forms stiff peaks, 5 to 7 minutes. Remove from heat. Beat in vanilla. (Makes about 5 cups.)

6. To assemble: Spread top of one cake layer with frosting. Top with remaining cake layer. Frost sides and top of cake.

Makes 12 servings.

246 CALORIES PER SERVING (WITHOUT FROSTING): 6 G PROTEIN; I G FAT; 58 G CARBOHYDRATE; 240 MG SODIUM; I MG CHOLESTEROL.

SEVEN-MINUTE FROSTING: 109 CALORIES PER SERVING: I G PROTEIN; O G FAT; 27 G CARBOHYDRATE; 42 MG SODIUM; O MG CHOLESTEROL.

Lemon Poppy Seed Cake Tart

	Butter or nonstick cooking spray for preparing pan
⅔	cup nonfat milk
2	tablespoons poppy seeds
1	jar (4 ounces) baby food pear puree
1	egg white, lightly beaten
¾	teaspoon vanilla
	Grated zest from 2 lemons
1⅓	cups cake flour
1	cup sugar
1	teaspoon baking powder
¼	cup lemon juice
½	cup raspberries
2	kiwi fruits, peeled and cut into thin wedges
10	small papaya balls
	Lemon zest rose (optional)
	Lemon leaves (optional)

1. Preheat oven to 375 degrees F. Lightly butter bottom and sides of 9-inch fluted indented fruit-tart mold or 9-inch round layer cake pan or spray with nonstick cooking spray. Combine nonfat milk and poppy seeds in small bowl. Let stand about 15 minutes. Stir in pear puree, egg white, vanilla and lemon zest.

2. Sift cake flour, ¾ cup sugar and baking powder into large bowl. Stir in nonfat-milk mixture just until blended. Pour into prepared pan. Bake about 20 minutes, or until wooden pick inserted in center comes out clean. Let cake cool in pan 5 minutes. Loosen edges and turn out onto wire rack with wax paper underneath.

3. Combine remaining ¼ cup sugar and lemon juice in small saucepan. Heat to boiling. Simmer about 1 minute, or until syrup is clear. Brush syrup over top and sides of cake while cake is still warm.

4. Place cake on serving platter. Arrange raspberries, kiwi and papaya on top. Garnish with lemon rose and several lemon leaves, if using.

Makes 8 servings.

206 CALORIES PER SERVING: 3 G PROTEIN; I G FAT; 47 G CARBOHYDRATE; 61 MG SODIUM; I MG CHOLESTEROL.

Beautifully different, this cake, which is made in a tart pan with an indented center, is a refreshing way to end a spring meal. Depending on the sweetness of the fruit you use for the topping, you may want to increase or decrease the sugar in the lemon syrup.

If desired, decorate the cake with fresh lemon leaves and/or a rose made from the peel: Starting at the tip of the fruit, peel off a long ¾-inch-wide strip of zest (yellow part only) and curl it tightly into a rose shape, securing it with a wooden pick. Cut off the excess pick.

To make papaya balls, scoop miniature balls from flesh of seeded papaya half, using ½-inch melon baller.

Banana Boston Creme Cake

It's a challenge to take the fat out of chocolate cake and still have a dessert with a light texture and a rich, chocolaty flavor. We did it by using cocoa powder, which is naturally low in fat, and by replacing most of the remaining fat with a combination of pureed bananas and nonfat egg substitute. We topped it with sliced bananas and a vanilla custard so pleasing to the palate you wouldn't know it's made with cornstarch and nonfat milk. If you want to cut the fat even further, omit the square of bittersweet chocolate used to make the design on top of the custard.

CUSTARD

¼	cup sugar
2	tablespoons cornstarch
1½	cups nonfat milk
½	cup thawed frozen nonfat egg substitute (equivalent to 2 eggs)
	2 teaspoons vanilla
¼	teaspoon banana extract

CAKE

	Butter or nonstick cooking spray for preparing pan
1	cup cake flour
¾	cup sugar
½	cup unsweetened cocoa powder
1	teaspoon baking soda
½	teaspoon baking powder
⅛	teaspoon salt
½	cup pureed banana (about 1 medium)
½	cup thawed frozen nonfat egg substitute (equivalent to 2 eggs)
1	teaspoon vanilla
3	tablespoons nonfat dry milk powder
1	cup hot water
1	banana, sliced
1	square (1 ounce) semisweet chocolate, melted
	Strawberries (optional)

1. Prepare Custard: Combine sugar and cornstarch in medium saucepan. Stir in nonfat milk until blended and smooth. Place over medium-low heat and bring to slow boil, stirring constantly. Stir some of hot liquid into egg substitute. Return all to pan and heat to simmering. Remove from heat and cool to room temperature. Stir in vanilla and banana extract. Cover and chill.

2. Prepare Cake: Preheat oven to 350 degrees F. Lightly butter bottom and sides of 9-inch indented fruit tart mold or spray with nonstick cooking spray. Sift together cake flour, sugar, cocoa powder, baking soda, baking powder and salt into large bowl.

3. In another bowl, whisk together pureed banana, egg substitute and vanilla. Combine nonfat dry milk and hot water, stirring until blended. Add banana mixture to dry ingredients, then add nonfat milk mixture. Stir just until blended. Pour into prepared pan.

4. Bake for about 20 minutes, or until wooden pick inserted in center comes out clean. Let cool in pan 5 minutes, then turn out onto wire rack to cool.

5. To assemble: Spread enough custard on cake to cover indented center. Arrange banana slices over custard. Pour remaining custard over top, spreading evenly. Drizzle melted chocolate in straight lines over custard. Using wooden pick, pull through chocolate lines to form web-like design. Serve with strawberries, if desired.

Makes 10 servings.

192 CALORIES PER SERVING: 6 G PROTEIN; 2 G FAT; 42 G CARBOHYDRATE; 188 MG SODIUM; 1 MG CHOLESTEROL.

Banana-Date Cake

DATE PUREE

1	cup pitted dried dates
6	tablespoons water
1	teaspoon vanilla

CAKE

	Butter or nonstick cooking spray for preparing pan
⅔	cup nonfat milk
2	teaspoons white vinegar
2⅓	cups all-purpose flour
1⅔	cups sugar
1¼	teaspoons baking powder
1¼	teaspoons baking soda
1	teaspoon salt
½	cup thawed frozen nonfat egg substitute (equivalent to 2 eggs)
1	egg white
1¼	cups mashed very ripe bananas (about 3 medium)
1	teaspoon vanilla
½	cup chopped walnuts (optional)
	Powdered sugar (optional)

1. Prepare Date Puree: Puree dates, water and vanilla in blender or food processor. (Makes about ¾ cup.)

2. Prepare Cake: Preheat oven to 350 degrees F. Lightly butter 12-cup Bundt pan or spray with nonstick cooking spray. Mix together nonfat milk and vinegar. Let stand until thickened. Sift together flour, sugar, baking powder, baking soda and salt in large mixing bowl. Stir to blend.

3. In another bowl, lightly beat egg substitute and egg white. Add to flour mixture with bananas, ¾ cup Date Puree, vinegar mixture, vanilla and walnuts, if using. Stir just until blended. Pour into prepared pan. Bake for 45 to 55 minutes, or until wooden pick inserted in center comes out clean. Let cake cool in pan 10 minutes. Unmold onto serving platter. Sprinkle with chopped walnuts and powdered sugar, if desired.

Makes 16 servings.

202 CALORIES PER SERVING: 4 G PROTEIN; I G FAT; 48 G CARBOHYDRATE; 243 MG SODIUM; I MG CHOLESTEROL.

This cake stays moist for days. Make sure that the dried fruit you're using has a fresh flavor and a soft, pliable texture. Although delicious on its own, this double-layer cake becomes sublime with an apricot brandy glaze. When topped with the season's best berries, it is an impressive finale.

Apricot Cake With Strawberries

APRICOT PUREE
1	cup pitted dried apricots
6	tablespoons water
1	teaspoon vanilla

CAKE
	Butter or nonstick cooking spray for preparing pans
2¾	cups all-purpose flour
1¾	cups sugar
2½	teaspoons baking powder
1¼	cups nonfat milk
½	cup thawed frozen nonfat egg substitute (equivalent to 2 eggs)
1½	teaspoons vanilla

APRICOT BRANDY GLAZE (OPTIONAL)
1	tablespoon sugar
1½	teaspoons cornstarch
½	cup canned apricot nectar
1½	teaspoons apricot brandy

9	tablespoons raspberry or strawberry preserves (optional)
8	large strawberries, sliced thin

1. Prepare Apricot Puree: Puree apricots, water and vanilla in blender or food processor. (Makes about ¾ cup.)

2. Prepare Cake: Preheat oven to 375 degrees F. Lightly butter bottoms and sides of two 8-inch round layer cake pans or spray with nonstick cooking spray. Sift together flour, sugar and baking powder into mixing bowl. Stir to blend. In another bowl, stir nonfat milk, ¾ cup Apricot Puree, egg substitute and vanilla until blended. Add liquid ingredients to dry ingredients, stirring just until blended. Do not overmix.

3. Pour into prepared pans. Bake for 25 to 30 minutes, or until wooden pick inserted in center comes out clean. Let cake cool in pans 5 minutes. Remove cakes from pans and cool on rack.

(continued on page 24)

4. Prepare Apricot Brandy Glaze, if using: Stir together sugar and cornstarch in small saucepan. Blend in apricot nectar. Heat to boiling, stirring constantly. Stir in apricot brandy. (Makes ½ cup.)

5. To assemble: Split each cake in half horizontally. Assemble four layers, spreading 3 tablespoons raspberry preserves between each layer, if using. Brush on enough Apricot Brandy Glaze to cover top of cake. Arrange strawberry slices in petal-like pattern on top. Brush remaining Apricot Brandy Glaze on strawberries and sides of cake.

Makes 12 servings.

255 CALORIES PER SERVING: 5 G PROTEIN; 0 G FAT; 59 G CARBOHYDRATE; 97 MG SODIUM; I MG CHOLESTEROL.

Lychee Marzipan Cake

Butter and flour for preparing pan
1 can (15 ounces) lychees
1¾ cups all-purpose flour
1½ cups plus 2 tablespoons sugar
2 teaspoons baking powder
½ teaspoon baking soda
¼ teaspoon salt
4 ounces almond paste
2 teaspoons almond extract
¼ cup light corn syrup
4 egg whites, slightly below room temperature
1 tablespoon cornstarch
1 mango, peeled, seeded and sliced or diced

1. Preheat oven to 350 degrees F. Lightly butter and flour nonstick 8-cup Bundt pan.

2. Drain lychees, reserving juice. Dice half the lychees and reserve remaining whole pieces for topping. Measure ¾ cup lychee juice and reserve remaining juice for topping.

3. Sift together flour, 1 cup sugar, baking powder, baking soda and salt into large mixing bowl. Crumble almond paste and add to flour mixture. Beat on low speed until blended. Beat in ¾ cup lychee juice, diced lychees, 1½ teaspoons almond extract and corn syrup just until blended.

4. In another mixing bowl, beat egg whites until frothy. Gradually add ½ cup sugar, beating until soft, smooth peaks form. Fold half the whites into batter until smooth and blended. Fold in remaining whites just to blend. Pour into prepared pan.

5. Bake for 30 minutes, or until wooden pick inserted in center comes out clean. Let cool in pan 5 minutes. Loosen from pan and unmold on wire rack to cool completely.

The compatible flavors of almond and lychee fruit unite in this Asian-inspired offering. Crumbled almond paste provides texture, but since it contains fat, only a small amount is used. To heighten its taste, we added a touch of almond extract.

Canned lychees are available wherever Asian foods are sold or in the Asian-products section of many supermarkets.

(continued on page 26)

6. Add enough water to reserved lychee juice to make 1⅓ cups. In small saucepan, combine remaining 2 tablespoons sugar and cornstarch. Whisk in lychee juice. Heat over medium heat until thickened, about 5 minutes. Stir in remaining ½ teaspoon almond extract and reserved whole lychees and mango pieces. Cool. Serve over top of cake.

Makes 12 servings.

276 CALORIES PER SERVING: 4 G PROTEIN; 3 G FAT; 59 G CARBOHYDRATE; 185 MG SODIUM; 0 MG CHOLESTEROL.

Pink Peppercorn Angel Food Cake

CAKE
1	cup all-purpose flour
1¼	cups sugar
½	teaspoon salt
2	teaspoons finely crushed pink peppercorns
2	cups egg whites (from 16 large eggs), slightly below room temperature
1½	teaspoons cream of tartar
2	teaspoons vanilla

RASPBERRY-MINT SAUCE
1	package (12 ounces) frozen raspberries
2	tablespoons sugar or to taste
1	cup fresh raspberries
1½	tablespoons chopped fresh mint leaves

The most delicate of all cakes is the light, airy angel food cake. This one has a surprise ingredient: crushed pink peppercorns. They give the cake a contrasting spicy bite. Minty raspberry sauce provides a sweet balance.

Pink peppercorns are available in specialty food stores.

1. Prepare Cake: Preheat oven to 325 degrees F. Sift together flour, ¾ cup sugar and salt onto wax paper. Stir in crushed pink peppercorns.

2. In large bowl, beat egg whites until foamy. Beat in cream of tartar. Gradually add remaining ½ cup sugar, beating only until soft, smooth peaks form. Beat in vanilla.

3. Sprinkle half the flour mixture over beaten whites and beat on low speed just until flour is mixed in. Repeat with remaining dry ingredients. Spread batter evenly in ungreased 10-inch tube pan. Remove air pockets by moving spatula up and down around center of pan.

4. Bake for 30 minutes, or until top is golden and wooden pick inserted in center comes out clean. Invert pan and cool completely. Remove cake from pan.

5. Prepare Raspberry-Mint Sauce: Puree frozen raspberries in blender until smooth. Stir in sugar to taste. Transfer to bowl and fold in whole fresh berries and mint. Serve with cake.

Makes 10 servings.

217 CALORIES PER SERVING: 7 G PROTEIN; 0 G FAT; 47 G CARBOHYDRATE; 231 MG SODIUM; 0 MG CHOLESTEROL.

Pineapple Meringue Torte

      Butter for preparing pans
2   cups cake flour
2   cups sugar
1   tablespoon baking powder
¾   teaspoon salt
1   can (1 pound 4 ounces) crushed pineapple, packed in water or
          syrup, undrained
2   teaspoons vanilla
6   egg whites, slightly below room temperature
½   cup chopped toasted cashew nuts
2½   cups low-fat whipped topping

1. Preheat oven to 350 degrees F. Lightly butter bottom and sides of three 9-inch round layer cake pans.

2. Sift together cake flour, 1⅓ cups sugar, baking powder and ½ teaspoon salt into large mixing bowl.

3. Drain pineapple, reserving 1 cup pineapple juice. Puree ½ cup of crushed pineapple and reserve remaining pineapple for frosting. Combine 1 cup reserved pineapple juice, ½ cup pureed pineapple and 1 teaspoon vanilla in small bowl. Quickly stir into dry ingredients.

4. Beat 3 egg whites until soft, smooth peaks form. Fold half into pineapple mixture until blended. Fold in remaining whites just until blended. Divide batter among prepared pans, spreading evenly.

5. Beat remaining 3 egg whites and remaining ¼ teaspoon salt until foamy. Gradually add remaining ⅔ cup sugar, beating until stiff but not dry. Fold in remaining 1 teaspoon vanilla and cashews. Spoon dollops of meringue evenly over three pans of cake batter. Spread meringue.

6. Bake for 20 to 25 minutes, or until wooden pick inserted in center comes out clean. Let cool in pans 5 minutes, then turn out onto wire racks to cool completely. Combine reserved pineapple and whipped topping. Spread between layers and over top and sides. Chill.

Makes 16 servings.

212 CALORIES PER SERVING: 3 G PROTEIN; 5 G FAT; 42 G CARBOHYDRATE; 199 MG SODIUM; 1 MG CHOLESTEROL.

Moist Rhubarb Coffee Cake

Nonstick cooking spray and butter for preparing pan
2   cups cake flour
1   teaspoon baking powder
1   teaspoon baking soda
½   teaspoon salt
1   cup plus 2 tablespoons light brown sugar, packed
¼   cup thawed frozen nonfat egg substitute (equivalent to 1 egg)
1   cup nonfat plain yogurt
½   cup unsweetened applesauce
1   teaspoon vanilla
3   cups coarsely chopped rhubarb

1. Preheat oven to 350 degrees F. Spray bottom of 9-inch square baking pan with nonstick cooking spray. Line bottom with parchment paper, then brush lightly with butter.

2. Sift together cake flour, baking powder, baking soda and salt into large bowl. Stir in 1 cup brown sugar.

3. Place egg substitute in small bowl. Stir in yogurt, applesauce and vanilla. Stir into flour mixture just until ingredients are blended. Quickly stir in rhubarb just until mixed. Turn into prepared pan.

4. Sprinkle top evenly with remaining 2 tablespoons brown sugar. Bake for 30 to 35 minutes, or until top springs back when touched. Cool in pan 10 minutes and turn out onto rack to cool completely.

Makes 9 servings.

224 CALORIES PER SERVING: 4 G PROTEIN; 1 G FAT; 51 G CARBOHYDRATE; 285 MG SODIUM; 1 MG CHOLESTEROL.

Yogurt and applesauce team up to enhance the texture of this cake, which has a lovely pink color in the crumb.

This lively jam cake, which is lightly spiced with cinnamon and topped with strawberries, is a wonderful pick-me-up any time of day. It is just as good without the cornflake topping, if you want to avoid the extra calories.

Breakfast Berry Jam Cake

Butter or nonstick cooking spray for preparing pan
1½ cups sifted all-purpose flour
3 teaspoons baking powder
1–2 teaspoons ground cinnamon
3 tablespoons low-fat butter spread, softened
½ cup sugar
½ cup thawed frozen nonfat egg substitute (equivalent to 2 eggs)
2 teaspoons vanilla
½ cup low-calorie currant, strawberry or raspberry jam
1½ cups chopped strawberries
1½ cups frosted flakes cereal
Powdered sugar (optional)
Whole or sliced strawberries or other berries for garnish
     (optional)
1 cup nonfat plain yogurt swirled with 1 tablespoon berry jam

1. Preheat oven to 350 degrees F. Lightly butter bottom and sides of 10-inch, 2-inch-deep round layer cake pan or spray with nonstick cooking spray. Resift flour with baking powder and cinnamon and set aside.

2. Cream butter spread and sugar until light. Beat in egg substitute and vanilla. Mix in ¼ cup jam. On low speed, mix in flour mixture. Fold in chopped berries. Swirl in remaining ¼ cup jam. Turn into prepared pan. Top with frosted flakes, lightly swirling some into batter.

3. Bake for 35 to 40 minutes, or until top is golden brown and wooden pick inserted in center comes out clean. Garnish with a light sprinkling of powdered sugar and additional fresh strawberries, if desired. Serve warm with yogurt-jam mixture.

Makes 12 servings.

156 CALORIES PER SERVING: 4 G PROTEIN; 2 G FAT; 32 G CARBOHYDRATE; 190 MG SODIUM; 1 MG CHOLESTEROL.

Summer Cakes

Fruit-Topped Yogurt Cheesecake

Light and smooth, this cheesecake isn't missing anything but calories and fat. Strained nonfat yogurt, low-fat ricotta cheese and egg whites are used in place of the traditional high-fat cream cheese. To reduce fat and cholesterol even further, use fat-free cottage cheese in place of ricotta. If you want crisper crumbs, sprinkle them on top of the cheesecake instead of on the bottom. Yogurt cheese, a thick, creamy, tangy yogurt concentrate, is a wonderful substitute for sour cream in many dessert recipes. Make it the day before you plan to bake the cake.

YOGURT CHEESE
1	quart nonfat plain yogurt

CHEESECAKE

Butter or nonstick cooking spray for preparing pan
1	cup finely crushed graham crackers or gingersnap cookies
1	cup low-fat ricotta cheese or fat-free cottage cheese
¾	cup sugar
⅓	cup nonfat milk
3	egg whites
2½	tablespoons cake flour
2–3	teaspoons vanilla
1	cup Fresh Fruit Puree
1½	cups hulled strawberries, mango pulp or other fresh fruit in season
2	tablespoons sugar or to taste
	Sliced fresh fruits or berries in season

1. Prepare Yogurt Cheese: Place yogurt in fine-mesh strainer lined with cheesecloth and place over deep bowl. Cover and refrigerate 6 to 8 hours, or until yogurt is thick and reduced to 2 cups. Discard liquid that has drained.

2. Prepare Cake: Preheat oven to 350 degrees F. Lightly butter bottom of 10-inch springform pan or spray with nonstick cooking spray. Sprinkle graham cracker or gingersnap crumbs in bottom of pan.

3. Combine 2 cups Yogurt Cheese, ricotta or cottage cheese, sugar, nonfat milk, egg whites, cake flour and vanilla in food processor bowl. Process only until smooth and blended. (Overblending will produce bubbles). Turn into prepared pan.

4. Bake for 40 to 45 minutes, or just until set. Cool on rack.

(continued on page 36)

5. Prepare Fresh Fruit Puree: Puree strawberries in blender with sugar until smooth.

6. Remove sides of springform pan. Cover cheesecake with plastic wrap and chill until serving time. Drizzle some Fresh Fruit Puree on top and/or garnish with fresh fruit. Serve with remaining fruit puree.

Makes 16 servings.

133 CALORIES PER SERVING: 6 G PROTEIN; 3 G FAT; 21 G CARBOHYDRATE; 91 MG SODIUM; 9 MG CHOLESTEROL.

Almost-No-Fat Baked Alaska

CHOCOLATE FUDGE ICE MILK
- ½ cup unsweetened cocoa powder
- ½ cup sugar
- 2 cups nonfat milk
- 1 teaspoon vanilla

ORANGE SORBET
- ½ cup sugar
- ½ cup fresh orange juice
   Grated zest from 1 orange
- 1 cup water

CAKE
- 1 cup cake flour
- 1 cup sugar
- ½ cup unsweetened cocoa powder
- 1 teaspoon baking powder
- ¾ cup nonfat milk
- 1 teaspoon vanilla
- 2 egg whites
- ¼ teaspoon cream of tartar

MERINGUE
- 5 egg whites, slightly below room temperature
- ½ teaspoon cream of tartar
- ½ cup sugar
- 1 teaspoon vanilla

   Strawberries or edible flowers (optional)

A fire-and-ice dessert, baked Alaska is an American classic. We replaced the traditional yellow cake with low-fat chocolate sponge cake. In place of the usual calorie-laden ice creams, we layered the cake with chocolate ice milk and orange sorbet. (If you're in a hurry, store-bought chocolate ice milk and orange sorbet may be used instead of homemade.) Then we covered it with meringue and baked it. None of the drama is lost.

Start the recipe the day before you plan to serve it; the unfrosted cake should be frozen overnight.

This recipe makes enough for two Baked Alaskas, or you can serve the extra cake with ice cream and fruit.

1. Prepare Chocolate Fudge Ice Milk: Combine cocoa powder and sugar in saucepan. Whisk in nonfat milk. Place over low heat, stirring just until cocoa and sugar are dissolved. Remove from heat. Stir in vanilla. Cool. Freeze in ice cream maker according to manufacturer's directions.

2. Prepare Orange Sorbet: Combine sugar, orange juice, zest and water in saucepan. Heat over medium heat, stirring just until sugar dissolves. Remove from heat and cool. Freeze in ice cream maker according to manufacturer's directions.

(continued on page 38)

3. Prepare Cake: Preheat oven to 375 degrees F. Line 15-x-10-inch jellyroll pan with parchment paper. Place 9-x-5-inch loaf pan in freezer to chill. Combine cake flour, ¾ cup sugar, cocoa powder and baking powder in large bowl.

4. In small bowl, stir together nonfat milk and vanilla. Stir into dry ingredients until blended. In another bowl, beat egg whites until frothy. Add cream of tartar. Continue beating until white and foamy.

5. Gradually beat in remaining ¼ cup sugar, beating until soft, smooth peaks form. Fold whites into cake batter. Spread batter into prepared jellyroll pan. Bake for about 10 minutes, or until wooden pick inserted in center comes out clean. Let cool in pan. Cover and freeze until ready to assemble. Cut cake into 4 rectangular pieces. (Freeze 2 pieces for another use.)

6. To assemble: Spoon Chocolate Fudge Ice Milk evenly into bottom of chilled loaf pan. Place 1 cake layer on top of Chocolate Fudge Ice Milk. Spoon Orange Sorbet evenly over cake layer. Top with another layer of cake. Cover and freeze overnight.

7. Just before serving cake, prepare Meringue: Beat egg whites until frothy. Add cream of tartar and continue beating until foamy. Gradually add sugar, beating until stiff but not dry. Beat in vanilla.

8. Preheat oven to 500 degrees F. Invert frozen cake onto foil-covered baking sheet or chilled ovenproof serving dish. Spread meringue over top and sides, being careful to seal all edges with meringue. Bake for 2 to 3 minutes, or until meringue is golden brown. Cut into 12 slices. Garnish with fresh strawberries or edible flowers, if using.

Makes 12 servings.

238 CALORIES PER SERVING: 7 G PROTEIN; I G FAT; 56 G CARBOHYDRATE; IO9 MG SODIUM; I MG CHOLESTEROL.

Mocha Fudge Sundae Cake

½ cup nonfat milk
4 teaspoons instant coffee powder
2 tablespoons melted butter or low-fat butter spread or canola oil
2 teaspoons vanilla
¾ cup plus 2 tablespoons sifted cake flour
1 cup sugar
¼ teaspoon salt (optional)
2 teaspoons baking powder
½ cup quick-cooking oats
¼ cup unsweetened cocoa powder
1¾ cups boiling water
2 tablespoons hazelnut liqueur, such as Frangelico or
      Kahlúa (coffee liqueur; optional)
      Fat-free ice cream or low-fat whipped topping (optional)
      Fresh or maraschino cherries or berries (optional)

1. Preheat oven to 350 degrees F. Heat ¼ cup nonfat milk. Stir in coffee powder to dissolve. Add remaining ¼ cup nonfat milk, melted butter and 1 teaspoon vanilla.

2. Resift cake flour with ½ cup sugar, salt and baking powder into large mixing bowl. Add milk mixture to dry ingredients, stirring with fork until blended. Mix in oats. Do not overmix.

3. Combine remaining ½ cup sugar, remaining 1 teaspoon vanilla and cocoa powder with boiling water. Mix well to dissolve cocoa. Stir in liqueur, if using. Pour into 8-inch square baking dish. Spoon batter on top in large spoonfuls. Bake for 40 to 45 minutes, or until top is crisp and sauce on bottom is bubbly. Let stand about 10 minutes.

4. Spoon into dessert dishes and spoon chocolate sauce from bottom of pan over each serving. If desired, serve with ice cream or a dollop of whipped topping and garnish with cherries or berries.

Makes 9 servings.

174 CALORIES PER SERVING: 3 G PROTEIN; 3 G FAT; 35 G CARBOHYDRATE; 110 MG SODIUM; 7 MG CHOLESTEROL.

You can call it hot fudge sundae cake, pudding cake or chocolate upside-down cake. In place of oats, substitute chopped dates, raisins or Rice Krispies. You may even throw in a bit of chopped almonds or shredded coconut. But no matter what you call it or how you vary the recipe, be sure to serve this dessert warm so that the pudding is smooth and saucy. Variation: For a double-fudge cake, add 2 tablespoons cocoa powder to flour mixture.

There is yellow squash hidden in this cake, but you'd never guess it. With its accent of chopped dates, it needs only a simple cinnamon-orange-tinged icing to dress it up. To add extra moistness and sweet citrus flavor, poke holes all over the warm surface and pour orange glaze over the cake. Adapted from a rich recipe with sour cream and pecans created by the late Bert Greene, this dessert has all of the flavor but none of the fat of the original. You can use crookneck, straight neck or even yellow zucchini, but be sure to select young squash with soft, thin skins.

Summer Date Cake

CAKE

	Butter and flour or nonstick cooking spray for preparing pan
½	pound yellow squash or yellow zucchini, trimmed
1	cup chopped pitted dried dates
2	teaspoons grated orange zest (from 1 orange)
2	cups all-purpose flour
2	teaspoons baking powder
1½	teaspoons baking soda
2	egg whites
½	cup thawed frozen nonfat egg substitute (equivalent to 2 eggs)
1¼	cups sugar
1	tablespoon vanilla
1	cup nonfat plain yogurt

ORANGE GLAZE (OPTIONAL)

3	tablespoons orange juice
2	tablespoons sugar

CINNAMON-ORANGE ICING

1	cup powdered sugar
2	tablespoons orange juice
1–2	tablespoons orange curaçao or Grand Marnier liqueur
1	teaspoon ground cinnamon
¼	cup finely chopped almonds (optional)

1. Prepare Cake: Preheat oven to 350 degrees F. Lightly butter and flour 8-cup Bundt cake pan or spray with nonstick cooking spray.

2. Finely chop squash in food processor. Combine squash with dates and orange zest in small bowl. Toss thoroughly with 2 tablespoons flour. Sift remaining flour with baking powder and baking soda and set aside.

3. Beat egg whites and egg substitute at medium speed in large mixing bowl until thick. Beat in sugar and vanilla. Beat in yogurt. Reduce speed to low and slowly add sifted dry ingredients, mixing only until blended. Fold in squash mixture. Pour batter into prepared pan.

4. Bake for 45 to 50 minutes, or until wooden pick inserted in center comes out clean. Cool on rack 10 minutes. Unmold onto cake platter.

5. Prepare Orange Glaze, if using: Stir together orange juice and sugar until smooth. Pierce surface of cake all over with skewer. Spoon glaze over warm cake, allowing it to soak in until cake is moist but not wet. Cool completely.

6. Prepare Cinnamon-Orange Icing: Combine powdered sugar, orange juice, liqueur and cinnamon in bowl. Mix until smooth. Use immediately. Drizzle as much icing as desired over cake and sprinkle with almonds, if using.

Makes 12 servings.

265 CALORIES PER SERVING: 5 G PROTEIN; I G FAT; 59 G CARBOHYDRATE; 203 MG SODIUM; I MG CHOLESTEROL.

Most recipes for upside-down cake call for lots of butter in the batter, but the only fat in this version is the tablespoon brushed on the pan. Nonetheless, the cake turns out tender and delicious. It is so easy that it can be made at the last minute. It is best served warm.

Pineapple Upside-Down Cake

1	tablespoon butter, softened
½	cup light brown sugar, packed
3	cans (8 ounces each) pineapple slices in unsweetened pineapple juice
9	maraschino cherries
1	cup cake flour
¾	cup sugar
1½	teaspoons baking powder
¼	cup thawed frozen nonfat egg substitute (equivalent to 1 egg)
½	teaspoon vanilla
¼	teaspoon coconut extract

1. Preheat oven to 350 degrees F. Brush bottom and sides of 9-inch square baking pan with butter. Sprinkle brown sugar over bottom of pan.

2. Drain pineapple slices, reserving ½ cup juice. Arrange 9 pineapple slices on brown sugar in pan. Place 1 maraschino cherry in center of each pineapple slice. Puree 2 pineapple slices. You will have ¼ cup puree. Reserve remaining sliced pineapple for another use.

3. Stir together cake flour, sugar and baking powder in large bowl. In another container, combine ¼ cup pureed pineapple, ½ cup reserved pineapple juice, egg substitute, vanilla and coconut extract. Quickly add liquid ingredients to dry ingredients, stirring just until blended. Do not overmix. Pour batter over pineapple in prepared pan, spreading lightly so as not to disturb pineapple.

4. Bake for 20 to 25 minutes, or until wooden pick inserted in center comes out clean and cake is golden brown. Do not overbake. Cool in pan about 5 minutes. Loosen cake around edges of pan. Place inverted serving platter over cake and turn both upside down. Shake gently, then remove pan. Slice into squares and serve warm.

Makes 9 servings.

208 CALORIES PER SERVING: 2 G PROTEIN; 1 G FAT; 49 G CARBOHYDRATE; 82 MG SODIUM; 3 MG CHOLESTEROL.

Golden Ginger Apricot Cake

This ginger-scented cake is studded with apricot halves filled with a mixture of cream cheese and candied ginger. As the cake bakes, some of the filling flows into the batter so you get a bit of cream cheese with every forkful.

Crystallized ginger is found in the spice section of the supermarket. For ginger juice, place one 2- or 3-inch piece of fresh ginger in a food processor. Process several seconds to puree. Wrap in cheesecloth and squeeze out the juice.

Butter for preparing pan
4 ounces light cream cheese
2 teaspoons minced crystallized ginger
½ teaspoon plus 1 cup sugar
1¼ teaspoons vanilla
8 whole fresh apricots, split, pits removed, or canned, drained
1⅓ cups cake flour
1 teaspoon baking powder
½ teaspoon baking soda
⅔ cup nonfat milk
½ cup apricot puree (from about 4–5 apricots) or baby-food apricot puree
¼ cup thawed frozen nonfat egg substitute (equivalent to 1 egg)
1 tablespoon fresh ginger juice
2 tablespoons finely crushed gingersnap cookies

1. Preheat oven to 375 degrees F. Lightly butter 10-inch round glass baking dish.

2. Blend together cream cheese, crystallized ginger, ½ teaspoon sugar and ¼ teaspoon vanilla. Spoon cream cheese mixture into center of each apricot half. Set aside.

3. Stir together cake flour, remaining 1 cup sugar, baking powder and baking soda in large bowl. In small bowl, whisk together nonfat milk, apricot puree, egg substitute, remaining 1 teaspoon vanilla and ginger juice until blended. Add apricot puree mixture to flour mixture, stirring just until blended. Pour into prepared baking dish. Push filled apricots into cake batter. Sprinkle with gingersnap crumbs.

4. Bake for about 20 minutes, or until wooden pick inserted in center of cake comes out clean. Serve warm with additional apricot puree, if desired.

Makes 12 servings.

158 CALORIES PER SERVING: 3 G PROTEIN; 2 G FAT; 33 G CARBOHYDRATE; 133 MG SODIUM; 4 MG CHOLESTEROL.

Kiwi Lime Torte

LIME CUSTARD
1¼   cups nonfat milk
¼   cup sugar
¼   cup thawed frozen nonfat egg substitute (equivalent to 1 egg)
3   tablespoons cornstarch
½   teaspoon grated lime zest

CAKE
1½   cups cake flour
1   cup plus 2 tablespoons sugar
1½   teaspoons baking powder
1   teaspoon baking soda
3   large kiwi fruits
¾   cup nonfat milk
½   cup thawed frozen nonfat egg substitute (equivalent to 2 eggs)
2   tablespoons fresh lime juice
1   teaspoon grated lime zest
2   egg whites, slightly below room temperature
¼   teaspoon cream of tartar

GELATIN GLAZE
1   tablespoon unflavored gelatin
½   cup water or clear fruit juice, such as apple or white grape
1   teaspoon sugar (optional)

2   large kiwi fruits
1   cup blackberries, raspberries or diced mangoes (optional)

1. Prepare Lime Custard: Combine nonfat milk, sugar, egg substitute and cornstarch in small saucepan. Stir until smooth. Place over low heat and cook, stirring constantly, until thickened. Cool. Cover and chill several hours until set. Stir in lime zest.

2. Prepare Cake: Preheat oven to 350 degrees F. Use nonstick 10-inch springform pan or line bottom and sides of ordinary springform pan with foil. Sift together cake flour, ½ cup sugar, baking powder and baking soda into large bowl. Make well in center.

Around the mid-1970s, a fuzzy fruit with a sunburst interior caught the fancy of gourmet chefs. The mildly sweet kiwi, once known as Chinese gooseberry, was renamed for the tiny kiwi bird from New Zealand, where the fruits were commercially grown. Thinly sliced kiwi, peeled and cut at the last minute, make a great garnish for this cake's custard layer.

(continued on page 48)

3. Peel 2 kiwi and puree. (You should have ½ cup.) Peel and dice 1 kiwi and reserve. Whisk together ½ cup kiwi puree, nonfat milk, egg substitute and lime juice. Add kiwi mixture to well in flour mixture and stir gently just until blended. Stir in lime zest. Do not overmix.

4. In another bowl, beat egg whites with cream of tartar until foamy. Slowly add remaining ½ cup plus 2 tablespoons sugar, beating until soft peaks form. Fold about one-third egg whites into kiwi batter until blended. Add remaining egg whites in two batches, folding gently until just blended. Fold in reserved diced kiwi. Turn into springform pan.

5. Bake for 35 minutes, or until wooden pick inserted in center comes out clean. Let cake cool completely. Do not remove from pan.

6. Prepare Gelatin Glaze: Sprinkle gelatin over water or juice and let stand 5 minutes to soften. Place over very low heat, stirring occasionally to dissolve gelatin, about 3 minutes. Stir in sugar, if desired. Cool until slightly thickened.

7. To assemble: Spread Lime Custard over cake in pan. Peel 2 kiwi fruits and slice ¼ inch thick. Arrange slices over custard. Garnish with well-drained blackberries, raspberries or diced mangoes, if using. Spoon Gelatin Glaze over fruit. Chill until gelatin sets. Remove torte from pan and foil.

Makes 16 servings.

139 CALORIES PER SERVING: 4 G PROTEIN; 0 G FAT; 31 G CARBOHYDRATE; 126 MG SODIUM; 1 MG CHOLESTEROL.

Here's a heavenly variation of the classic cake made with cocoa. Who says it needs frosting? The cake will be gone before you can make one. Light and airy, angel cake achieves its volume mainly from the steam that evaporates during baking and passes through air cells that have been whipped into the egg whites. A common mistake is to overbeat the egg whites until they are stiff and dry, making it difficult to fold in the other ingredients. Furthermore, the overextended air cells will deflate during baking, resulting in small cakes. Beat the whites only until the peaks are soft, smooth and shiny.

Dark Angel Cake

¼   cup plus 2 tablespoons sifted cake flour
¾   cup unsweetened cocoa powder
1½   cups plus 3 tablespoons sugar
½   teaspoon salt
1½   cups egg whites (from 11–12 eggs), slightly below room
        temperature
1½   teaspoons cream of tartar
2   teaspoons vanilla

1. Preheat oven to 325 degrees F. Resift cake flour with cocoa powder, ¾ cup sugar and salt.

2. In large bowl, beat egg whites on low speed 1½ minutes, or until frothy. Sprinkle cream of tartar over whites. Beat on medium speed until white and foamy. Slowly add remaining sugar, beating 2 to 3 minutes, or until soft (not stiff), smooth peaks form.

3. Sprinkle one-third cocoa mixture and vanilla over egg whites. Fold in with rubber spatula, keeping spatula under surface of batter as you fold. Repeat two more times with remaining cocoa mixture. Do not overfold. Pour into ungreased 9- or 10-inch tube pan.

4. Bake in lower third of oven about 35 to 45 minutes, or until cake springs back when touched and wooden pick inserted in center comes out clean. Remove from oven and invert tube pan on counter. Let cool in pan about 2 hours before removing.

Makes 16 servings.

109 CALORIES PER SERVING: 4 G PROTEIN; I G FAT; 25 G CARBOHYDRATE; 129 MG SODIUM; O MG CHOLESTEROL.

California Avocado-Cake With Dates

Butter or nonstick cooking spray for preparing pan
1½ cups cake flour
1⅓ cups sugar
1½ teaspoons baking soda
½ teaspoon ground cinnamon
½ teaspoon ground nutmeg
½ teaspoon ground allspice
½ teaspoon salt
1 cup mashed avocado (from about 1½ avocados)
½ cup thawed frozen nonfat egg substitute (equivalent to 2 eggs)
⅓ cup nonfat milk
1 cup chopped pitted dried dates
Powdered sugar
Slivered dates for garnish (optional)

1. Preheat oven to 325 degrees F. Lightly butter nonstick 9-inch square baking pan or spray with nonstick cooking spray.

2. Sift together cake flour, sugar, baking soda, cinnamon, nutmeg, allspice and salt into large bowl. Blend together avocado, egg substitute and nonfat milk in small bowl. Stir avocado mixture into dry ingredients along with dates until blended. Spread evenly in prepared pan.

3. Bake for 25 to 30 minutes, or until wooden pick inserted in center comes out clean. Cool in pan 5 minutes. Invert on wire rack and cool completely. Sprinkle lightly with powdered sugar. Garnish top with a few slivers of dates, if desired.

Makes 12 servings.

212 CALORIES PER SERVING: 3 G PROTEIN; 3 G FAT; 46 G CARBOHYDRATE; 211 MG SODIUM; 0 MG CHOLESTEROL.

The natural oil in the avocado makes a healthful substitute for butter, keeping this cake moist.

For an easy decorative finish, you can use a paper doily. Press the doily firmly on top of the cake and sprinkle powdered sugar over it. Carefully lift off the doily and the lacy pattern will remain.

Southwest Chayote Cake With Pepita Praline

	Butter or nonstick cooking spray for preparing pan
2	cups sifted flour
2	teaspoons ground cinnamon
1	tablespoon ancho or pasilla chili powder or other hot chili powder
2	teaspoons baking powder
1	teaspoon baking soda
½	teaspoon salt
½	cup light brown sugar, packed
1	egg yolk
¼	cup tequila or rum
⅔	cup light corn syrup
2	cups shredded peeled and seeded chayote, undrained (from about 2–3 chayotes)
	Grated zest from 1 orange
3	egg whites, slightly below room temperature
½	cup sugar

ORANGE GLAZE

	Juice from 1 orange
1	teaspoon butter
1	tablespoon sugar or to taste

PEPITA PRALINE

2–3	tablespoons shelled pumpkin seeds (pepitas)
½	cup sugar
2	tablespoons water

1. Preheat oven to 350 degrees F. Line 9-x-13-inch baking pan with parchment paper. Lightly butter or spray with nonstick cooking spray.

2. Resift flour with cinnamon, chili powder, baking powder, baking soda and salt into large bowl. Stir in brown sugar. Make well in center and add egg yolk, tequila or rum, corn syrup, chayote and orange zest. Stir just until blended.

(continued on page 54)

This is a perfect ending for a menu with a Southwest theme. Chayote, the vegetable "pear" cultivated by the Aztecs and Mayans long before Columbus, has a juicy pulp that turns to a sweet starch during baking. It lends a nice moistness and tender texture to this unusual cake. There's no need to frost it; instead, each serving gets a little pumpkin-seed brittle for crunch.

The spiciness of the cake may be increased by adding an extra ½ tablespoon chili powder.

3. Beat egg whites until foamy. Slowly add sugar, beating until soft, smooth peaks form. Fold half the beaten whites into batter until smooth. Gently fold in remaining whites until completely blended. Turn batter into prepared pan. Bake for 30 minutes, or until wooden pick inserted near center comes out clean. Cool cake in pan on wire rack, cut into squares and remove from pan.

4. Prepare Orange Glaze: Combine orange juice, butter and sugar in small saucepan. Place over medium heat and cook 3 to 5 minutes. Using skewer, poke holes evenly in cake and spoon on warm glaze. Let cool on rack.

5. Prepare Pepita Praline: Lightly toast pumpkin seeds in 10-inch nonstick skillet sprayed with nonstick cooking spray. Remove seeds onto plate. Spray same skillet with nonstick cooking spray. Add sugar and water and cook, without stirring, over medium-high heat until sugar starts to change color. Reduce heat to medium-low and heat until sugar is completely melted to light golden color, stirring occasionally or shaking pan. Add pumpkin seeds, stirring just to coat seeds evenly. Flatten seeds with spoon or lightly shake pan so seeds are in single layer. Cool caramel in skillet until firm. Pry praline off skillet, reheating briefly if it doesn't come out of pan. Break into small uneven shards. Cut cake in squares and garnish with shards of Pepita Praline.

Makes 16 servings.

196 CALORIES PER SERVING: 3 G PROTEIN; I G FAT; 42 G CARBOHYDRATE; 190 MG SODIUM; 14 MG CHOLESTEROL.

Fall Cakes

Blueberry-Pear Cake in Crème Anglaise

½   cup orange marmalade
4   pears, peeled, cored, each cut in 8 wedges
1   cup fresh blueberries
2   cups all-purpose flour
1¼   cups sugar
3   teaspoons baking powder
½   cup thawed frozen nonfat egg substitute (equivalent to 2 eggs)
1   jar (6 ounces) baby food pear puree
1   cup nonfat milk
2   tablespoons butter, melted
2   teaspoons vanilla

CRÈME ANGLAISE
2   cups nonfat milk
¼   cup sugar
¼   cup thawed frozen nonfat egg substitute (equivalent to 1 egg)
3   tablespoons cornstarch
1   teaspoon vanilla

1. Preheat oven to 350 degrees F. Brush bottom of nonstick 11-inch round baking pan with orange marmalade. Arrange pear wedges, tips outward, in two concentric circles in prepared pan. Fill spaces between fruit with 2 to 3 blueberries. Reserve remaining berries for batter.

2. Sift flour, sugar and baking powder into large bowl. Combine egg substitute, pear puree, nonfat milk, melted butter and vanilla in small bowl. Stir until blended. Make well in dry ingredients and stir in liquid mixture. Gently fold in reserved blueberries. Carefully pour batter over fruits in pan.

3. Bake for about 25 minutes until golden brown, or until wooden pick inserted in center comes out clean. Cool 5 minutes. Loosen cake around edges of pan. Carefully invert onto large shallow platter.

(continued on page 58)

4. Prepare Crème Anglaise: Whisk together nonfat milk, sugar, egg substitute and cornstarch in small saucepan until smooth. Place over medium-low heat and cook until thickened, whisking constantly. Stir in vanilla. Pour sauce around cake. Serve warm or at room temperature.

Makes 16 servings.

230 CALORIES PER SERVING: 4 G PROTEIN; 2 G FAT; 50 G CARBOHYDRATE; 118 MG SODIUM; 5 MG CHOLESTEROL.

Caramel Apple Cake, Tarte Tatin Style

1¾	cups sugar
2	tablespoons water
2	tablespoons butter
1½	teaspoons almond extract
3	pounds apples (preferably green-skinned Golden Delicious or Fuji apples), peeled and cored
1	cup cake flour
1½	teaspoons baking powder
¼	cup thawed frozen nonfat egg substitute (equivalent to 1 egg)
½	cup unsweetened apple juice
2	tablespoons Amaretto (almond liqueur)
2	egg whites, slightly below room temperature
1	cup low-fat whipped topping (optional)

1. Combine 1 cup sugar and water in heavy, deep ovenproof 10-inch skillet. Bring to boil over medium heat, stirring occasionally. Cook to light caramel stage or pale amber color, stirring occasionally. Remove from heat. Swirl in butter and ½ teaspoon almond extract.

2. Cut each apple into 4 wedges. Arrange about three-fourths apples in tight single layer over caramel. Cut remaining apple wedges in halves and place on top of first apple layer. Cover skillet and cook apples over medium-low heat until they exude juices, about 10 minutes. Uncover skillet and increase heat to medium. Continue cooking about 25 to 30 minutes, or until caramel syrup is thick, but not burned (adjust heat to low if caramel is cooking too fast). Baste apples occasionally with caramel syrup, using baster or spoon. Remove from heat and set aside.

3. Preheat oven to 350 degrees F. Sift cake flour with baking powder and ½ cup plus 2 tablespoons sugar in large bowl. Make well in center. In another bowl, whisk egg substitute, apple juice, remaining 1 teaspoon almond extract and Amaretto. Add to well in flour mixture, slowly stirring into dry ingredients just to blend.

Loosely modeled upon the classic French favorite, this version replaces the rich pastry tart shell of the original with a nonfat cake flavored with almond. The apples are cooked with sugar and a minuscule amount of butter until they have become golden; they develop an intense flavor that enriches the upside-down cake. If you don't tell your guests this is a low-fat dessert, they'll feel guilty asking for second helpings.

(continued on page 60)

4. Beat egg whites until foamy. Add remaining 2 tablespoons sugar, beating to soft, smooth peaks. Fold small amount of batter into egg whites, then fold back mixture into remaining batter. Pour over apples in skillet.

5. Bake for 25 to 30 minutes, or until wooden pick inserted in center comes out clean.

6. Cool 5 minutes in skillet. Loosen cake around edges. Place platter over skillet and carefully invert pan, shaking gently to release cake onto platter. Spoon any remaining glaze over top. Serve with low-fat whipped topping, if desired.

Makes 12 servings.

242 CALORIES PER SERVING: 2 G PROTEIN; 3 G FAT; 54 G CARBOHYDRATE; 82 MG SODIUM; 5 MG CHOLESTEROL.

Fresh Ginger Gingerbread

Butter or nonstick cooking spray for preparing pan
1½ cups all-purpose flour
1 teaspoon ground ginger
1 teaspoon ground cinnamon
½ teaspoon baking powder
½ teaspoon baking soda
½ teaspoon salt
⅛ teaspoon ground cloves
2 jars (2 ½ ounces each) baby food pear puree
½ cup dark molasses
½ cup boiling water
¼ cup light brown sugar, packed
¼ cup thawed frozen nonfat egg substitute (equivalent to 1 egg)
1 teaspoon peeled, grated fresh ginger

WARM CARAMEL PEARS (OPTIONAL)
4 medium pears or apples, peeled, cored and sliced ½ inch thick
⅓ cup sugar
1 tablespoon butter
1 tablespoon brandy
1 teaspoon lemon juice

Low-fat whipped topping (optional)
Chopped crystallized ginger (optional)

1. Preheat oven to 350 degrees F. Lightly butter 8-inch round layer cake pan or spray with nonstick cooking spray. Sift together flour, ground ginger, cinnamon, baking powder, baking soda, salt and cloves into mixing bowl. Stir to blend. Add pear puree, molasses, boiling water, brown sugar, egg substitute and ginger. Stir just until blended. Pour into prepared pan.

2. Bake for 25 to 30 minutes, or until wooden pick inserted in center comes out clean. Let cake cool 10 minutes in pan. Invert onto wire rack and cool.

3. Prepare Warm Caramel Pears, if using: Combine pears, sugar, butter, brandy and lemon juice in skillet. Cook over medium-high heat, stirring occasionally, for 10 to 15 minutes, or until sugar starts to caramelize to light amber color and pears are tender but firm. Serve warm.

4. Serve slices of warm gingerbread with caramel pears and top with whipped topping and crystallized ginger, if using.

Makes 6 servings.

231 CALORIES PER SERVING: 4 G PROTEIN; I G FAT; 53 G CARBOHYDRATE; 296 MG SODIUM; 0 MG CHOLESTEROL.

Maple Corn Flan Cake

Flan cakes, composed of a rich flan of whole eggs and cream over a chiffon cake, may seem difficult to make at first but really aren't. If you've never made one before, you may be reluctant to pour the cake batter over the flan liquid. Don't worry: the two mixtures will form two distinct layers just as they should. This corn cake covered with maple-tapioca flan offers a unique compromise: a minute amount of the fat of the original with a delicious flavor and excellent texture.

FLAN

¾	cup sugar
2	tablespoons water
¾	cup thawed frozen nonfat egg substitute (equivalent to 3 eggs)
2	cups nonfat milk
1	teaspoon maple flavoring
1	teaspoon vanilla
2	tablespoons instant tapioca

CORN CAKE BATTER

1	can (8 ounces) whole kernel corn
1	cup sifted cake flour
¾	cup sugar
2	teaspoons baking powder
¼	teaspoon salt
1	tablespoon corn or canola oil
1	teaspoon vanilla
3	egg whites, slightly below room temperature
¼	teaspoon cream of tartar
1	cup nonfat plain yogurt sweetened to taste (optional)

1. Prepare Flan: Preheat oven to 350 degrees F. Heat 10-inch round, 2-inch-deep cake pan in oven while you caramelize sugar.

2. Heat ½ cup sugar with 2 tablespoons water in heavy 10-inch skillet over medium-high heat until sugar starts to change color. Stir and reduce heat to medium-low. Heat just until lightly golden, stirring occasionally. Quickly pour into hot baking pan (use oven mitts to handle hot pan), tilting pan to spread caramel evenly over bottom. Cool.

3. Whisk egg substitute, nonfat milk, remaining ¼ cup sugar, maple flavoring and vanilla in bowl until smooth. Stir in tapioca and set aside.

4. Prepare Corn Cake Batter: Drain corn kernels and add water to liquid to make ½ cup. Reserve half of corn kernels and puree remaining

(continued on page 66)

half in blender, adding ¼ cup corn liquid. Combine puree with remaining corn liquid and remaining corn kernels. Resift cake flour with ¼ cup sugar, baking powder and salt into bowl. Make well in center and add corn mixture, oil and vanilla. Stir until blended.

5. Beat egg whites with cream of tartar until foamy. Slowly add remaining ½ cup sugar, beating until soft, smooth peaks form. Add half of whites to batter and fold until completely blended. Fold in remaining whites just until blended. Use immediately.

6. Stir tapioca flan mixture again to blend, then pour into caramel in pan. Carefully pour in Corn Cake Batter. Place cake pan in larger shallow baking pan and place in oven. Pour hot water into larger pan to reach about one-third up side of round cake pan. Bake about 45 minutes, or until knife inserted in center comes out clean. Cool 15 minutes on rack. Loosen cake around edges of pan. Turn upside down into large serving platter. Serve with nonfat yogurt, if desired.

Makes 12 servings.

180 CALORIES PER SERVING: 5 G PROTEIN; 1 G FAT; 39 G CARBOHYDRATE; 204 MG SODIUM; 1 MG CHOLESTEROL.

Apple Spice Cake

Butter or nonstick cooking spray for preparing pan
<table>
<tr><td>2</td><td>cups all-purpose flour</td></tr>
<tr><td>1¼</td><td>cups sugar</td></tr>
<tr><td>1½</td><td>teaspoons ground cinnamon</td></tr>
<tr><td>1¼</td><td>teaspoons baking soda</td></tr>
<tr><td>½</td><td>teaspoon salt</td></tr>
<tr><td>¼</td><td>teaspoon ground cloves</td></tr>
<tr><td>¼</td><td>teaspoon ground nutmeg</td></tr>
<tr><td>½</td><td>cup thawed frozen nonfat egg substitute (equivalent to 2 eggs)</td></tr>
<tr><td>½</td><td>cup unsweetened applesauce</td></tr>
<tr><td>⅓</td><td>cup apple juice</td></tr>
<tr><td>1</td><td>teaspoon vanilla</td></tr>
<tr><td>2</td><td>cups chopped peeled apples</td></tr>
<tr><td>¼</td><td>cup light brown sugar, packed</td></tr>
<tr><td>¼</td><td>cup chopped walnuts (optional)</td></tr>
</table>

1. Preheat oven to 350 degrees F. Lightly butter 8-inch square baking pan or spray with nonstick cooking spray.

2. Sift together flour, sugar, cinnamon, baking soda, salt, cloves and nutmeg into large mixing bowl. Stir to blend.

3. In another bowl, stir together egg substitute, applesauce, apple juice and vanilla. Stir into dry ingredients just until blended. Fold in apples. Spoon batter into prepared pan.

4. Combine brown sugar and walnuts, if using. Sprinkle evenly over top of batter. Bake for 40 to 45 minutes, or until wooden pick inserted in center comes out clean.

Makes 9 servings.

257 CALORIES PER SERVING: 4 G PROTEIN; I G FAT; 61 G CARBOHYDRATE; 254 MG SODIUM; O MG CHOLESTEROL.

Everything's warm and appealing about this old-fashioned apple cake: the sweet, fragrant spices, the apples and the brown sugar and walnut topping. Pears may be used in place of apples.

Cranberry Upside-Down Cake

This is an impressive dessert for a Thanksgiving repertoire that's very pretty and not difficult to make. The orange cake is extremely moist and the citrus complements the bittersweet cranberries.

Butter or nonstick cooking spray for preparing pan
2 cups cranberries, washed and picked over
1¾ cups sugar
½ cup water
1 cup cake flour
1½ teaspoons baking powder
½ cup unsweetened applesauce
¼ cup thawed frozen nonfat egg substitute (equivalent to 1 egg)
¼ cup nonfat milk
¼ cup fresh orange juice
1 teaspoon grated orange zest
½ teaspoon vanilla
1 cup low-fat whipped topping
1 tablespoon orange liqueur

1. Preheat oven to 375 degrees F. Lightly butter bottom and sides of 9-inch round layer cake pan or spray with nonstick cooking spray.

2. Combine cranberries, 1 cup sugar and water in medium saucepan. Bring to boil. Reduce heat and simmer until slightly thickened to syrupy consistency, about 10 minutes. Pour into prepared pan. Cool to room temperature.

3. Sift together cake flour, remaining ¾ cup sugar and baking powder into large bowl. In another bowl, stir applesauce, egg substitute, nonfat milk, orange juice, orange zest and vanilla. Stir into dry ingredients just until blended. Pour over cranberry mixture.

4. Bake for 25 to 30 minutes, or until wooden pick inserted in center comes out clean. Let cake cool in pan about 5 minutes.

5. Loosen cake around edges of pan. Place inverted serving platter over cake and turn both upside down. Shake gently, then remove pan. Serve warm with whipped topping blended with orange liqueur.

Makes 10 servings.

210 CALORIES PER SERVING: 2 G PROTEIN; 2 G FAT; 49 G CARBOHYDRATE; 69 MG SODIUM; I MG CHOLESTEROL.

Carrot-Fig Cake

FIG PUREE

2	cups dried figs
¾	cup water
2	teaspoons vanilla

CAKE

	Butter or nonstick cooking spray for preparing pan
1	can (8 ounces) crushed pineapple, undrained
½	cup thawed frozen nonfat egg substitute (equivalent to 2 eggs)
2	egg whites
2	cups all-purpose flour
2	cups sugar
2	teaspoons baking powder
2	teaspoons ground cinnamon
1½	teaspoons baking soda
1	teaspoon salt
2	cups peeled, grated carrots
1	cup dark seedless raisins
½	cup chopped walnuts (optional)
1	cup powdered sugar for glaze (optional)

1. Prepare Fig Puree: Puree figs, water and vanilla in blender or food processor. (Makes about 1½ cups.)

2. Prepare Cake: Preheat oven to 350 degrees F. Lightly butter 9-x-13-inch baking pan or spray with nonstick cooking spray. Drain pineapple, reserving 2 tablespoons juice. Lightly beat together egg substitute and egg whites in small bowl.

3. Sift together flour, sugar, baking powder, cinnamon, baking soda and salt into large mixing bowl. Stir to blend. Add 1½ cups Fig Puree, beaten eggs, carrots, crushed pineapple, raisins and walnuts, if using. Stir until blended. Pour into prepared pan.

Most people think a carrot cake is healthful. What they forget is that most carrot cakes are made with a great amount of oil: in the high-fat original of this recipe, there are 1½ cups. Replace the oil with pureed figs, and you reduce the percentage of calories from fat from 50 percent to 4 percent. The wonderful aroma of this cake may tempt you to eat it straight out of the oven, but wait if you can. It keeps well and it is even better the next day.

(continued on page 70)

4. Bake for 35 to 40 minutes, or until wooden pick inserted in center comes out clean.

5. If making glaze, blend together powdered sugar and 2 tablespoons reserved pineapple juice until smooth and of pourable consistency. Drizzle over warm cake. Cut into squares and remove from pan.

Makes 24 servings.

173 CALORIES PER SERVING: 3 G PROTEIN; I G FAT; 42 G CARBOHYDRATE; 184 MG SODIUM; O MG CHOLESTEROL.

S'Mores Cakes

Butter or nonstick cooking spray for preparing pans
⅔ cup cake flour
2½ cups graham cracker crumbs
2 teaspoons baking powder
1 cup nonfat milk
½ cup unsweetened applesauce
1 teaspoon vanilla
3 egg whites, slightly below room temperature
¼ teaspoon cream of tartar
½ cup sugar
2 cups miniature marshmallows
¼ cup mini chocolate chips

1. Preheat oven to 350 degrees F. Lightly butter two 8-inch spring-form cake pans or 8-inch round layer cake pans lined with foil, or spray pans with nonstick cooking spray.

2. Stir together cake flour, graham cracker crumbs and baking powder into medium bowl. In another bowl, combine nonfat milk, applesauce and vanilla. Add to dry ingredients, stirring just until blended.

3. Beat egg whites until frothy. Add cream of tartar and continue beating until thick and foamy. Gradually add sugar, beating until soft, smooth peaks form. Fold half egg-white mixture into batter until blended. Fold in remaining whites until just blended. Divide batter between prepared pans, spreading evenly.

4. Bake for 15 to 20 minutes, or until wooden pick inserted in centers comes out clean. Preheat broiler.

5. Sprinkle marshmallows, then chocolate chips over tops of hot cakes. Place under broiler to brown lightly. Let cool slightly. Remove from pans and serve warm.

Makes 2 cakes (16 servings).

149 CALORIES PER SERVING: 3 G PROTEIN; 2 G FAT; 31 G CARBOHYDRATE; 130 MG SODIUM; 0 MG CHOLESTEROL.

Remember s'mores? We ate them in Girl Scouts, melting marshmallows and chocolate over the campfire, then sandwiching them between graham crackers. These low-fat s'mores are perfect for Halloween. Watch out, kids, adults will gobble them up too.

This recipe makes two cakes. Wrap the second one in foil and store in the freezer for up to 1 month.

Harvest Pumpkin Cake

CAKE

	Butter or nonstick cooking spray for preparing pans
1	cup dried currants
1	cup canned pumpkin (not pie filling)
½	cup unsweetened applesauce
½	cup thawed frozen nonfat egg substitute (equivalent to 2 eggs)
½	cup nonfat milk
1	teaspoon vanilla
2	cups cake flour
2	teaspoons baking powder
1½	teaspoons ground cinnamon
1	teaspoon ground ginger
½	teaspoon baking soda
½	teaspoon ground cloves
1½	cups dark brown sugar, packed

CREAM CHEESE FROSTING

3	ounces light cream cheese
1	cup sifted powdered sugar
½	teaspoon vanilla

1. Prepare Cake: Preheat oven to 375 degrees F. Butter 9-x-13-inch baking pan or spray with nonstick cooking spray. Place currants in small bowl. Let stand in warm water to cover until plumped. Drain.

2. Combine pumpkin, applesauce, egg substitute, nonfat milk and vanilla in bowl and blend well.

3. Sift together cake flour, baking powder, cinnamon, ginger, baking soda and cloves into large bowl. Stir in brown sugar. Add pumpkin mixture and drained currants, stirring just until blended. Pour into prepared pan, spreading evenly. Bake for 20 minutes, or until wooden pick inserted in center comes out clean. Cool in pan on rack to room temperature.

4. Prepare Frosting: Blend cream cheese, powdered sugar and vanilla in food processor. Spread on cooled cake.

Makes 24 servings.

141 CALORIES PER SERVING: 2 G PROTEIN; 1 G FAT; 31 G CARBOHYDRATE; 80 MG SODIUM; 1 MG CHOLESTEROL.

Winter Cakes

Coffee Cream Roulade With Cashew Crunch

Coffee Cream Filling
1½	cups nonfat milk
3	tablespoons sugar
	Pinch salt
2½	teaspoons instant coffee powder
¼	cup thawed frozen nonfat egg substitute (equivalent to 1 egg)
2	tablespoons cornstarch
1½	teaspoons vanilla
½	carton (8 ounces) low-fat whipped topping

Cake
	Nonstick cooking spray, butter and flour for preparing pan
2–4	tablespoons powdered sugar
¾	cup all-purpose flour
1¼	cups sugar
½	teaspoon salt
1	cup egg whites (from 7–8 large eggs), slightly below room temperature
1	teaspoon cream of tartar
1½	teaspoons vanilla

Cashew Praline
⅓	cup sugar
1½	tablespoons water
1	teaspoon butter
3	tablespoons chopped toasted cashews
⅓	cup low-fat whipped topping (optional)
	Raspberries for garnish

1. Prepare Coffee Cream Filling: Heat 1 cup nonfat milk, sugar and salt in saucepan over low heat. Stir in coffee powder to dissolve. Whisk remaining ½ cup nonfat milk with egg substitute and cornstarch until smooth. Slowly add to saucepan and heat until thickened, about 3 min-

Everyone loves old-fashioned ice cream cake rolls. The jellyroll for a dessert like this is usually the classic spongecake, which is made with egg yolks and therefore high in cholesterol. This version, made without yolks, is really angel food cake filled with a sumptuous coffee "cream." A little crunch is added with pralines made from cashews, one of the lower-fat nuts. In place of whipped topping, a small amount of coffee filling may be reserved and used for piping on top of roll. (See photograph on the front cover.)

(continued on page 76)

utes, whisking frequently. Stir in vanilla. Chill until thickened, about 2 to 4 hours. Fold in whipped topping. Chill until ready to use.

2. Prepare Cake: Preheat oven to 350 degrees F. Spray 15-x-10-inch jellyroll pan with nonstick cooking spray. Line with sheet of foil or parchment paper and brush lightly with butter. Sprinkle lightly with flour. Sprinkle powdered sugar lightly over clean tea towel and set aside. Sift flour with ½ cup sugar and salt and set aside.

3. Beat egg whites with cream of tartar on low speed 1½ minutes, or until frothy. Increase speed to medium-high. Beat until white and foamy. Gradually add remaining ¾ cup sugar, beating until soft (not stiff), smooth peaks form. Beat in vanilla.

4. Sprinkle with one-third the flour mixture and fold in. Add remaining flour mixture in two batches, folding just until incorporated. Turn batter into prepared pan and spread evenly.

5. Bake for 12 to 15 minutes, or until top springs back when touched in center. Loosen cake from pan using sharp, thin knife along sides of pan. Invert cake onto sugared towel and roll up while warm. Cool completely before unrolling and filling.

6. Prepare Cashew Praline: Stir sugar and water in medium skillet. Heat over medium-high heat, without stirring, until color starts to change. Stir. Reduce heat to low. Heat until sugar caramelizes to light golden color, stirring occasionally. Remove from heat and stir in butter, then nuts. Pour into baking sheet. Cool. Chop or coarsely grind in food processor.

7. To assemble: Unroll cake and place on foil-lined tray. Spread with Coffee Cream Filling. Sprinkle with half the Cashew Praline. Roll up. Wrap in foil. Freeze several hours on tray. Using pastry tube fitted with star tip, pipe a few rows of whipped topping on top of roll. Garnish with raspberries. Cut into 12 slices and serve on plates dusted with remaining ground Cashew Praline.

Makes 12 servings.

228 CALORIES PER SERVING: 5 G PROTEIN; 5 G FAT; 44 G CARBOHYDRATE; 203 MG SODIUM; 2 MG CHOLESTEROL.

Lemon Dream Cake

A lemon curd filling and a billowy, seven-minute frosting add flair to this simple, versatile, all-occasion cake that may be served for special parties or just to surprise the family.

LEMON CURD

1½	cups sugar
7	tablespoons cornstarch
½	teaspoon salt
2	cups boiling water
¼	cup thawed frozen nonfat egg substitute (equivalent to 1 egg)
¼	cup fresh lemon juice
1	tablespoon butter
1	tablespoon grated lemon zest

CAKE

	Butter or nonstick cooking spray for preparing pan
2⅔	cups cake flour
1½	cups sugar
2	teaspoons baking powder
1	teaspoon baking soda
1	cup nonfat milk
1	cup unsweetened applesauce
½	cup thawed frozen nonfat egg substitute (equivalent to 2 eggs)
2	teaspoons vanilla
⅓	cup fresh lemon juice
	Grated zest from 2 lemons
2	egg whites, slightly below room temperature

FLUFFY LEMON FROSTING

¾	cup sugar
2	tablespoons cold water
2	egg whites
¼	teaspoon cream of tartar
½	teaspoon vanilla
¼	teaspoon lemon extract
1	tablespoon sliced almonds, toasted

1. Prepare Lemon Curd: Stir together sugar, cornstarch and salt in top of double boiler. Stir in boiling water until blended. Heat mixture to boiling until clear and thickened, stirring frequently. Place over simmer-

(continued on page 78)

ing water in double boiler and heat 10 minutes, uncovered. Add a little hot liquid to egg substitute, stirring until blended. Return to pan and cook 2 minutes. Stir in lemon juice, butter and lemon zest. Transfer to bowl and cool to room temperature. (Makes about 2½ cups.)

2. Prepare Cake: Preheat oven to 350 degrees F. Lightly butter bottom and sides of two 9-inch round layer cake pans or spray with nonstick cooking spray. Sift together cake flour, sugar, baking powder and baking soda into large bowl.

3. In another bowl, combine nonfat milk, applesauce, egg substitute, vanilla, lemon juice and zest. Stir to blend.

4. Beat egg whites until stiff but not dry. Quickly fold in applesauce mixture. Fold into dry ingredients just until moistened. Divide batter between prepared cake pans. Bake for 25 to 30 minutes, or until wooden pick inserted in centers comes out clean. Let cool in pans 5 minutes. Remove cakes from pans to wire racks to cool.

5. Prepare Fluffy Lemon Frosting: Combine sugar, cold water, egg whites and cream of tartar in top of double boiler. Beat 30 seconds with electric mixer until blended. Beat about 7 minutes over simmering water until stiff peaks are formed. Remove from heat, stir in vanilla and lemon extract. (Makes about 2½ cups.)

6. To assemble: Split each cake layer in half. Assemble 4 layers, spreading ½ cup Lemon Curd on top of each of 3 layers and remaining 1 cup on top layer. Frost sides of cake with Fluffy Lemon Frosting. Arrange almonds around top of cake.

Makes 12 to 16 servings.

378 CALORIES PER SERVING: 5 G PROTEIN; 2 G FAT; 89 G CARBOHYDRATE; 279 MG SODIUM; 3 MG CHOLESTEROL.

Cappuccino Chocolate Cheesecake

1¼   cups chocolate wafers, crushed (22 wafers)
⅛   teaspoon ground cinnamon
1   package (8 ounces) light cream cheese
1   cup sugar
1   cup unsweetened cocoa powder, plus more for garnish
½   cup thawed frozen nonfat egg substitute (equivalent to 2 eggs)
2½   cups nonfat sour cream substitute
2   tablespoons coffee liqueur
1   teaspoon vanilla

This chocolate cheesecake is so smooth and silky that no one guesses it is low in fat. Even the crust is made without butter. Serve the dessert chilled, or if you want a more pronounced chocolate flavor, at room temperature.

1. Preheat oven to 350 degrees F. Stir together wafer crumbs and cinnamon. Pat into bottom of 9-inch springform pan.

2. Beat cream cheese until light and fluffy. Beat in sugar and cocoa powder. Beat in egg substitute. Stir in 2 cups sour cream substitute, coffee liqueur and vanilla. Turn into prepared pan. Bake for about 30 minutes, or until set.

3. Spread remaining ½ cup sour cream substitute evenly over top. Return to oven 1 minute to glaze top. Cool to room temperature, then chill thoroughly, covered. Remove from springform pan. Just before serving, dust top with cocoa powder in decorative pattern, if desired.

Makes 16 servings.

159 CALORIES PER SERVING: 5 G PROTEIN; 5 G FAT; 25 G CARBOHYDRATE; 200 MG SODIUM; 5 MG CHOLESTEROL.

Chocolate Raspberry Cake

This is a dark, dense, yet tender chocolate cake. Although it contains banana, the predominant flavor is chocolate. Since this recipe makes three layers, we cut the cake into thin wedges.

CAKE

	Nonstick cooking spray and butter for preparing pans
2	cups all-purpose flour
1	cup unsweetened cocoa powder
1½	cups sugar
2	teaspoons baking soda
1	teaspoon baking powder
¼	teaspoon salt
1	cup banana puree (from 2 medium bananas)
½	cup thawed frozen nonfat egg substitute (equivalent to 2 eggs)
2	teaspoons vanilla
2	cups hot water
⅓	cup nonfat dry milk powder
2	egg whites, slightly below room temperature

FUDGE FROSTING

1	can (14 ounces) sweetened condensed milk
½	cup unsweetened cocoa powder
1	teaspoon vanilla
9	tablespoons raspberry preserves
	Mint sprig
¾	cup fresh raspberries

1. Prepare Cake: Preheat oven to 350 degrees F. Spray bottom of three 8-inch round layer cake pans with nonstick cooking spray, then line with parchment paper and lightly butter. Sift together flour, cocoa powder, sugar, baking soda, baking powder and salt into large bowl.

2. In another bowl, combine pureed bananas, egg substitute and vanilla and blend well. Blend together hot water and nonfat dry milk. Stir into banana mixture. Beat egg whites until stiff but not dry. Gently stir banana mixture into whites. Fold mixture into dry ingredients. Divide batter among prepared pans.

3. Bake for about 15 minutes, or until wooden pick inserted in centers comes out clean. Let cool in pans 5 minutes. Turn out onto wire racks to cool. Split each cake layer in half to make 6 layers.

4. Prepare Fudge Frosting: Combine condensed milk and cocoa powder in medium saucepan. Heat over low heat, stirring constantly, until thickened and glossy. Remove from heat. Stir in vanilla.

5. To assemble: Place one cake layer on serving platter. Spread 3 tablespoons raspberry preserves on top. Cover with second cake layer and spread top evenly with ¼ cup Fudge Frosting. Cover with third cake layer and spread with another 3 tablespoons preserves. Cover with fourth cake layer and spread with another ¼ cup Fudge Frosting. Place fifth cake layer on top and spread with remaining 3 tablespoons preserves. Cover with last cake layer and frost top and sides of cake with remaining frosting. Garnish top of cake with mint sprig and several raspberries. Arrange raspberries around base of cake.

Makes 16 servings.

291 CALORIES PER SERVING: 8 G PROTEIN; 4 G FAT; 61 G CARBOHYDRATE; 226 MG SODIUM; 9 MG CHOLESTEROL.

Four-Spice Cake

DATE PUREE
1   cup pitted dried dates
6   tablespoons water
2   teaspoons vanilla

CAKE

   Butter or nonstick cooking spray for preparing pan
1   cup golden raisins
2   cups cake flour
1   teaspoon baking soda
1   teaspoon ground nutmeg
1   teaspoon ground cinnamon
½   teaspoon ground allspice
½   teaspoon ground cloves
½   teaspoon salt
1   cup light brown sugar, packed
2   egg whites
1   cup buttermilk

ORANGE SYRUP
¼   cup water
2   tablespoons sugar
¼   teaspoon orange flower water (optional)
1   orange, sliced thinly

1. Prepare Date Puree: Combine dates, water and vanilla in blender and puree until smooth. (Makes scant 1 cup.)

2. Prepare Cake: Preheat oven to 350 degrees F. Lightly butter 8-cup Bundt pan or spray with nonstick cooking spray. Soak raisins in hot water to cover until plump. Drain. Sift together cake flour, baking soda, nutmeg, cinnamon, allspice, cloves and salt into large bowl. Stir in brown sugar.

3. Beat egg whites lightly in another bowl. Stir in buttermilk and Date Puree. Stir into dry ingredients along with drained raisins just until blended. Pour into prepared pan.

4. Bake for 35 to 45 minutes, or until wooden pick inserted in center comes out clean. Cool 10 minutes in pan, then invert on serving plate.

5. Prepare Orange Syrup: Combine water, sugar and orange flower water, if using, in small saucepan. Bring to boil. Add orange slices and simmer 1 minute. Strain and reserve orange slices for garnish. Brush syrup over warm cake and decorate with orange slices.

Makes 12 servings.

245 CALORIES PER SERVING: 4 G PROTEIN; I G FAT; 59 G CARBOHYDRATE; 197 MG SODIUM; I MG CHOLESTEROL.

Persimmon Pudding Cake

Butter or nonstick cooking spray for preparing pan
1   cup all-purpose flour
1   cup sugar
1   teaspoon ground cinnamon
¼   teaspoon ground nutmeg
¼   teaspoon salt
2   teaspoons baking soda
2   teaspoons warm water
1   cup peeled and pureed persimmon (from 3–4 very ripe fruits)
½   cup thawed frozen nonfat egg substitute (equivalent to 2 eggs)
3   tablespoons brandy
2   tablespoons butter, melted
1   teaspoon vanilla
1   cup dark seedless raisins
¼   cup chopped walnuts

1. Preheat oven to 325 degrees F. Lightly butter 5-cup tube mold or spray with nonstick cooking spray.

2. Sift together flour, sugar, cinnamon, nutmeg and salt into large bowl.

3. Blend together baking soda and warm water in another bowl. Stir in persimmon puree along with egg substitute, brandy, butter and vanilla. Stir persimmon mixture into dry ingredients until almost blended. Stir in raisins and walnuts. Pour batter into prepared pan.

4. Bake for about 1½ hours, or until wooden pick inserted near center comes out clean. Let stand about 5 minutes, then unmold onto serving dish.

Makes 10 servings.

254 CALORIES PER SERVING: 4 G PROTEIN; 4 G FAT; 51 G CARBOHYDRATE; 260 MG SODIUM; 6 MG CHOLESTEROL.

Persimmons begin to come into the marketplace as early as mid-September and are available all through the holiday season. Thick and intensely orange, the pureed fruits provide succulence to this dark pudding cake. Select a beautifully sculptured metal mold for an elegant holiday cake and enhance it with a circle of miniature fresh fruits or a winter compote. A warm slice served with cappuccino is especially appealing on a cold winter day.

Prune Pudding Cake

This one-pot cake was adapted from a favorite recipe of Los Angeles Times food editor Ruth Reichl. It's a cross between a pudding and a cake and it is mixed, boiled and baked in the same pot. We added plum puree to this low-fat version. Serve warm.

3 cups pitted prunes, chopped (about 1½ packages, 12 ounces each)
2 cups strong brewed coffee
½ cup plum puree (from 1 large plum, peeled and pitted)
1 cup sugar
1½ teaspoons ground cinnamon
½ teaspoon ground cloves
½ teaspoon salt
2 teaspoons baking soda
2 cups all-purpose flour

YOGURT CREAM TOPPING
1 cup low-fat whipped topping
1 cup nonfat plain yogurt

1. Preheat oven to 350 degrees F. Combine prunes, coffee, plum puree, sugar, cinnamon, cloves and salt in 12-inch round heavy metal pan or ovenproof skillet about 2½ inches deep. Heat to boiling, stirring constantly. Simmer about 3 minutes, stirring frequently. Remove from heat. Add baking soda, stirring until blended. Stir in flour until incorporated.

2. Bake for about 25 to 30 minutes, or until wooden pick inserted in center comes out clean.

3. Prepare Yogurt Cream Topping: Blend together whipped topping and yogurt. Serve over wedges of warm cake.

Makes 20 servings.

153 CALORIES PER SERVING: 3 G PROTEIN; 1 G FAT; 36 G CARBOHYDRATE; 147 MG SODIUM; 1 MG CHOLESTEROL.

Brandied Fig Cake

FIG PUREE
½	cup dried figs
3	tablespoons water
1	teaspoon vanilla

CAKE
	Butter or nonstick cooking spray for preparing pan
1	tablespoon plus ½ cup yellow cornmeal
1	cup diced dried figs
½	cup brandy
½	cup fresh orange juice
1¼	cups cake flour
½	cup sugar
1	teaspoon baking powder
¼	teaspoon baking soda
½	teaspoon salt
½	cup thawed frozen nonfat egg substitute (equivalent to 2 eggs)
1	teaspoon fresh ginger juice
½	cup pine nuts, toasted

BROWN SUGAR GLAZE
⅓	cup light brown sugar, packed
1	tablespoon butter
½	teaspoon water
¼	teaspoon vanilla

1. Prepare Fig Puree: Combine figs, water and vanilla in food processor and blend until smooth. (Makes ¾ cup.)

2. Prepare Cake: Preheat oven to 350 degrees F. Lightly butter bottom of 9-inch round layer cake pan or spray with nonstick cooking spray. Sprinkle with 1 tablespoon cornmeal, tilting pan to coat evenly on bottom and sides.

3. Combine diced figs, brandy and orange juice in small saucepan. Heat to simmer. Cook 1 minute. Let cool to room temperature. Sift together cake flour, remaining ½ cup cornmeal, sugar, baking powder, baking soda and salt into large bowl.

The dried fig puree not only replaces the fat in the cake, but it gives a fabulous taste. Yellow cornmeal adds a distinctive texture, while the brown sugar glaze drizzled on top enhances sweetness. To reduce the fat further, cut down on the pine nuts or omit them completely.

Crystallized ginger is found in the spice section of the supermarket. For ginger juice, place one 2- or 3-inch piece of fresh ginger in food processor. Process several seconds into a puree. Wrap in cheesecloth and squeeze out the juice.

This makes a great holiday gift.

(continued on page 90)

4. In small bowl, combine ¾ cup Fig Puree, cooled brandy mixture, egg substitute and ginger juice. Add to dry ingredients along with pine nuts, stirring just until blended. Pour batter into prepared pan.

5. Bake for 30 to 35 minutes, or until wooden pick inserted in center comes out clean. Cool in pan about 5 minutes. Remove cake to wire rack to cool completely.

6. Prepare Brown Sugar Glaze: Combine brown sugar and butter in saucepan over medium heat. Heat until blended and sugar is dissolved, stirring occasionally. Stir in water and vanilla. Add additional water if necessary for good consistency. Drizzle over cake.

Makes 12 servings.

253 CALORIES PER SERVING: 5 G PROTEIN; 4 G FAT; 46 G CARBOHYDRATE; 162 MG SODIUM; 3 MG CHOLESTEROL.

Cinnamon-Apple-Oatmeal Cake

Butter or nonstick cooking spray for preparing pan

1	tablespoon plus ½ cup quick-cooking oats
1	tablespoon plus 1½ cups sifted all-purpose flour
¼	cup light brown sugar, packed
3	teaspoons ground cinnamon
3–4	tablespoons low-fat butter spread, softened
1	cup sugar
4	egg whites
2	teaspoons vanilla
2	teaspoons baking powder
1	teaspoon baking soda
1	teaspoon ground allspice
¾	cup nonfat milk
1½	pounds firm apples, peeled, cored and cut into ½-inch dice (4 cups)
1	cup low-fat whipped topping blended with 1 tablespoon rum or apple brandy (optional)

1. Preheat oven to 350 degrees F. Butter nonstick 12-x-7-inch baking pan or spray with nonstick cooking spray. Or line pan with parchment paper and butter lightly. Combine 1 tablespoon oats, 1 tablespoon flour, brown sugar and 1 teaspoon cinnamon in small bowl and set aside.

2. Cream low-fat butter spread and sugar in mixing bowl until fluffy. Add egg whites, beating 4 to 5 minutes. Beat in vanilla.

3. Resift remaining 1½ cups flour with remaining 2 teaspoons cinnamon, baking powder, baking soda and allspice. Alternately add to egg white mixture with nonfat milk, stirring just until blended.

4. Reserve 1 cup diced apples. Fold remaining apples and remaining ½ cup oats into batter. Turn into prepared pan. Scatter reserved apples on top, then sprinkle brown sugar mixture over. Bake for 35 to 40 minutes, or until wooden pick inserted in center comes out clean. Serve warm from pan with whipped topping, flavored with rum, if desired.

Makes 9 servings.

274 CALORIES PER SERVING: 5 G PROTEIN; 3 G FAT; 59 G CARBOHYDRATE; 246 MG SODIUM; 1 MG CHOLESTEROL.

This homey apple cake is made with oats and cinnamon. Choose any firm apple you like. Granny Smiths add a touch of tartness. If you prefer one of the sweeter varieties, choose green-skinned Golden Delicious or Fuji apples; both hold up well in baking without turning mushy. Although this dessert stands on its own merits, you can dress it up a bit. A dollop of light whipped topping blended with a splash of rum or Calvados makes it doubly good.

Blond Fruitcake

Butter or nonstick cooking spray for preparing pan
1 pound candied pineapple
¾ pound dried apricots
½ pound dried peaches
1¾ cups all-purpose flour
1 cup sugar
½ teaspoon baking powder
1 cup unsweetened applesauce
1 cup thawed frozen nonfat egg substitute (equivalent to 4 eggs)
1 tablespoon vanilla
1 tablespoon lemon extract
Orange liqueur

1. Preheat oven to 250 degrees F. Lightly butter 9-inch tube pan or spray with nonstick cooking spray.

2. Cut pineapple, apricots and peaches into ½-inch dice and combine in large bowl. Add ¼ cup flour, tossing to coat fruit. Sift together remaining 1½ cups flour, sugar and baking powder into another bowl.

3. In small bowl, combine applesauce, egg substitute, vanilla and lemon extract. Stir into dried-fruit mixture. Add flour mixture, stirring until blended. Spoon batter into prepared pan.

4. Bake for 3 hours, or until wooden pick inserted in center comes out clean. Let cool in pan on wire rack. Remove from pan. Soak cheesecloth in liqueur. Wrap cake in cheesecloth. Store in covered container in refrigerator for several weeks or longer before serving, occasionally adding more liqueur to cake.

Makes 20 servings.

235 CALORIES PER SERVING: 3 G PROTEIN; 2 G FAT; 57 G CARBOHYDRATE; 27 MG SODIUM; 0 MG CHOLESTEROL.

To replace the fat in this holiday fruitcake, we used applesauce and added lots of mixed dried fruit. Long, slow baking keeps the cake moist. Prepare it at least a month before the holidays to allow sufficient time for aging. A sprinkling of ruby-red pomegranate seeds over the top adds sparkle for the holidays.

A county fair recipe winner was the inspiration for this "drunken" honey raisin cake. We left in the rum called for but replaced the butter with nonfat yogurt. Don't be lured into eating the cake right out of the oven; its texture improves and its flavor mellows after a day or so of aging. If desired, add nuts to the cake batter.

Tipsy Honey Tea Ring

Butter and flour for preparing pan
1   cup dark seedless raisins
¾   cup dark rum
2   cups all-purpose flour
1   teaspoon baking soda
2   teaspoons baking powder
2   teaspoons ground cinnamon
1   teaspoon ground coriander or anise seeds
½   teaspoon salt
1   egg yolk, beaten
½   cup nonfat plain yogurt
Grated zest from 1 large orange
1   cup plus 2 tablespoons honey
4   egg whites, slightly below room temperature
½   cup dark brown sugar, packed
1   tablespoon sesame seeds, toasted

1. Lightly butter 7-cup ring mold and dust with flour. Soak raisins in rum in covered bowl. Sift together flour, baking soda, baking powder, cinnamon, coriander or anise seeds and salt into large bowl. Make well in center and stir in egg yolk, yogurt, orange zest and 1 cup honey. Stir in raisins with the rum.

2. Beat egg whites until foamy. Gradually add brown sugar, beating until soft, smooth peaks form. Fold half the whites into honey batter until blended. Fold in remaining egg whites. Turn into prepared pan.

3. Bake for 1 hour and 10 minutes. Let cool in pan 5 to 10 minutes. Remove to wire rack and spoon remaining 2 tablespoons honey over top. Sprinkle with sesame seeds. Cut in thin slices.

Makes 20 servings.

179 CALORIES PER SERVING: 3 G PROTEIN; I G FAT; 37 G CARBOHYDRATE; I47 MG SODIUM; II MG CHOLESTEROL.

Index